Advance praise for *Harborless*

"In Cindy Hunter Morgan's elegant collection, *Harborless*, the unique power of historic poetry is on full display. These meticulous and striking poems balance imagination and fact to explore the complex maritime narratives of the Great Lakes. The result is an important and refreshing book full of unexpected histories and wonder."

— Adrian Matejka, author of *The Big Smoke*

"Here, a shipload of cast iron stoves slips to the bottom of the lake, where it will rest forever among the teacups, the crankshafts, the revolvers, and the bones of sailors. On one level, Cindy Hunter Morgan's *Harborless* is a deft and moving chronicle of forty shipping catastrophes in the Great Lakes, described with loving attention to detail, to the tiny particulars that create our sense of a whole story. But on a greater level, this is also a book about the transience of human experience, the vagaries of memory, and the forces that buffet all of us, often wildly and violently, during and after our lives. *Harborless* is a brilliant first book, one that will continue to haunt me."

— Kevin Prufer, co-curator of The Unsung Masters Series

D0769586

HARBORLESS

MADE IN MICHIGAN WRITERS SERIES

General Editors
Michael Delp
Interlochen Center for the Arts

M. L. Liebler
Wayne State University

Advisory Editors
Melba Joyce Boyd
Wayne State University

Stuart Dybek
Western Michigan University

Kathleen Glynn

Jerry Herron
Wayne State University

Laura Kasischke
University of Michigan

Thomas Lynch

Frank Rashid
Marygrove College

Doug Stanton

Keith Taylor
University of Michigan

A complete listing of the books in this series can be found online at wsupress.wayne.edu

HARBORLESS

POEMS BY

Cindy Hunter Morgan

Wayne State University Press
Detroit

ISBN 978-0-8143-4242-8 (paperback)
ISBN 978-0-8143-4243-5 (e-book)

Library of Congress Control Number: 2016943657

Publication of this book was made possible by a generous gift from
The Meijer Foundation. Additional support provided by Michigan Council
for Arts and Cultural Affairs and National Endowment for the Arts.

Designed and typeset by Libby Bogner, Good Done Daily
Composed in Fazeta Serif and Fazeta Sans

Wayne State University Press
Leonard N. Simons Building
4809 Woodward Avenue
Detroit, Michigan 48201-1309

Visit us online at wsupress.wayne.edu

CONTENTS

ACKNOWLEDGMENTS

Thanks are due to the editors of the following publications, in which some of the poems first appeared:

Blue Lyra Review:
"Columbia, 1859"

Burntdistrict:
"Deckhand: Color Theory," "Deckhand: Scent Theory," and "Deckhand: Dream Theory"

Cheat River Review:
"Francisco Morazan, 1960" and *"Alpena, 1880"*

Fogged Clarity:
"Erie, 1841"

Midwestern Gothic:
"Henry Steinbrenner, 1909"

Museum of Americana:
"J. Oswald Boyd, 1936," "Rouse Simmons, 1912," and *"Sidney E. Smith, Jr., 1972"*

Potomac Review:
"Carl D. Bradley, 1958" and *"Wisconsin, 1929"*

Salamander:
"Henry Clay, 1851" and *"Omar D. Conger, 1922"*

Michigan Composer Philip Rice set *"Rouse Simmons, 1912"* to music. That work was premiered at Michigan State University's Residential College in the Arts and Humanities in February of 2015.

Three poems (*Chicora*, 1895; *Pheonix*, 1847; and *Waldo*, 1913) also appear in a 2015 interview on *Murder Ballad Monday*, a blog hosted by Sing Out!

❀

Thanks to my family: my son Tommy, and my parents, Tom and Nancy
Hunter. Thanks also to my sister and my aunts, uncles, and cousins. Thanks
to Dennis Hinrichsen for friendship, and for reading all of these poems in their
early stages and helping me think about the shape of this book. Thanks to
Steve Germic for friendship and a good title. Thanks to Kevin Prufer and Cate
Marvin, who shared meaningful feedback on a few of these poems. Thanks to
John Beck, Bill Castanier, and Thomas Lynch, who shared their enthusiasm
for this project. Many thanks to Annie Martin at Wayne State University
Press for believing in my manuscript. Gracious appreciation for friends who've
shared support in various and important ways: Maureen Abood, Don Albrecht,
Ken Bigger, Eileen Cleary, Guillermo Delgado, Stacy Dickert-Conlin, Shanna
Draheim, Suzanne Edison, Jodi Eppinga, Robbie Gamble, Karin Gottshall,
Karen Henry, Mani Iyer, Annette Kopachik, Geralyn Lasher, Kevin Leckrone,
Michael Mercurio, Carol Pratt, Sarah Preisser, Andrea Read, Philip Rice, Robin
Silbergleid, and Anita Skeen. Thanks, too, for Michigan State University's
RCAH Center for Poetry, an extraordinary resource for poets and those who
love poetry. I'm also tremendously grateful for the resources of the East Lansing
Public Library and the Michigan State University Library, and thankful for
libraries everywhere.

HARBORLESS

DECKHAND: SCENT THEORY

When he climbed up the deck ladder
that first morning, his shirt still smelled
of his mother's wash line:
Dreft and sunshine.

Now what he breathes is rain
and ore, deck paint, grease,
engine oil, boiler exhaust,
steam.

Mornings there is coffee.
Sometimes he pours a bit
on the cuff of his sleeve
so later he can press his nose in it.

Still, what blows in from the deck
is metallic and sharp-edged:
wind scraped by steel
mixed with hydraulic fluid.

It is not enough to air
the passageways, which reek of sweat:
glandular and primal,
a condensation of what is repressed.

His own body is slick with it.
At night he peels
his clothes off
and drops them in a pile,

dark, stagnant puddle
of stained cotton,
cesspool of sweat turning
to mildew.

HENRY STEINBRENNER, 1909
St. Marys River

His childhood was edged with fence lines
and planted with hollyhocks,
which his mother sometimes cut
and brought inside to a table
in the kitchen where the floor never
pitched and dishes never slid.
Once a year, his father took him fishing.
He imagined the line as a kind of taproot,
a fish as a kind of tuber.
After he shipped out on the *Henry Steinbrenner*,
he saw plow furrows in the wake of the boat—
a dark, churned field that did not smell
of the earth. Every day, he looked beyond
that wake for the shade of the maple tree
where he liked to rest at noon with a jug
of buttermilk. He muttered in his sleep,
too wet to plow, too wet to plow,
and woke one night to a violent thump.
Thrown from a horse, he thought,
but the chief engineer was yelling
to put out the fires so the boilers
would not explode. His head
was waterlogged. He shook it, thinking
something would sprinkle out—rain
from his mother's watering can.
Someone ordered him to pull burning coals
from the fire boxes, which he did
because he had always loved
simple tasks. He piled coals
on the steel deck, carrying them almost gently,
pretending they were newly hatched chicks.

W. W. ARNOLD, 1869
Lake Superior

In the November storm,
>   the hull of the schooner ran
>   aground
near the mouth of the
>   Two-Hearted River.
The mast was gone.
>   Forty feet
>   above the lake, on a bluff,
the debris:
>   cabin roof, furniture, bedding,
>   a wrecked yawl.
Ten corpses
>   strewn on the beach.
>   A trapper found them,
>   but would not go near them.
He only reckoned
>   they were dead.
>   In Munising,
>   he unpacked
his pelts and his news, all of it
stiff.
>   People talked
>   about what to do,
and four men in the Masonic Order
>   left on snowshoes
>   to find their brother's body.
There was no straight course,
>   and the men
>   pulled
in different directions,
the tips of their snowshoes pointing
>   north, south, east, west
>   until they stamped circles in the snow.
At night,
>   they camped and stared

at constellations,

trying to fix

their position,

but the sky was useless,

a broken compass.

It took days to reach the wreck,

and by then there were not any bodies,

only remnants of things

the living once used.

They found bits

of canvas

and clothing embedded in ice,

which they dug out and saved,

brushing away snow

and lifting

a frayed cuff of a shirt

or the thin heel of a sock

as though pulling

a clump of wildflowers

from soil—

each thread dangling

like a delicate root.

ERIE, 1841
Lake Erie

In August, they left Buffalo
on a steamboat full of immigrants.
Homeless and groundless,
passengers floated in beds
or hovered over game tables
or gripped deck railings,
steadying themselves.
Everyone wobbled, queasy and uncertain.
On the deck, two demijohns of turpentine
pitched and rolled like dice.

When the boilers exploded,
some passengers burned in their bunks
while others threw luggage in the water
and jumped in after it, hoping
their cracked satchels full of family pictures
would float them.
They clung to sepia faces
of mothers and grandmothers,
which stared, unblinking, into disaster.

One man, twenty, climbed
off the deck onto a side-wheel.
He sat on a spoke,
his hair freshly cut by the ship barber,
a picture of his girl in his vest pocket,
her head bobbing gently
as the ship rose and fell
as though she was nestled beside him
high on a ferris wheel,
rocking above a new country.

CHICORA, 1895
Lake Michigan

Cups and plates spilled
into the lake, a terrible clattering
lost among splitting timbers.

The fury was so great
it exceeded sound, numbed
the ears of a coal passer,

who paused, mute on the tilted deck,
and spotted the dishes in torrent and foam.
They looked as though they were soaking

in soap suds. A dipper from a gravy bowl
spinning on the surface, cream
from a milk crock swirling in liquid

as dark as the sky. Some men
he knew had already tasted it—
were sinking beneath a new milky way.

ROUSE SIMMONS, 1912
Lake Michigan

The Rouse Simmons was one of many vessels employed in the Christmas tree trade
and it is from this simple business that the aging schooner derived its nickname, the
Christmas Tree Ship. . . . When it sank, the ice-covered schooner went down with 17
crew members and a load of 5,000 or more trees.
—Benjamin J. Shelak, *Shipwrecks of Lake Michigan*

Fishermen wondered why they caught balsam and spruce,
their nets full of forests, not fish.
What they hooked smelled like Christmas, diluted.
Each bough dripped with last winter's tinsel.

Their nets full of forests, not fish,
men wanted trees to writhe and flip.
Each bough dripped with last winter's tinsel.
Needles were pin bones of fish.

Men wanted trees to writhe and flip.
What they netted could not even float.
Needles were pin bones of fish,
every trunk an ossified spine, broken.

What they netted could not even float.
They caught what had already died,
every trunk an ossified spine, broken—
each one as tall as a man.

They caught what had already died.
Those trees were meant for Chicago,
each one as tall as a man,
but they were four months late for Christmas.

Those trees were meant for Chicago,
for families who waited on docks,
but they were four months late for Christmas.
The ship sunk in November.

For families who waited on docks,
what they hooked smelled like Christmas, diluted.
The ship sunk in November.
Fishermen wondered why they caught balsam and spruce.

PHILADELPHIA, 1893

Lake Huron

The ship sank with a load
of cast-iron stoves, which tumbled,

lopsided, through white foam,
green water, teal water, water

as dark as coal, then darker.
From deck to lake floor,

they dropped 200 feet,
plummeting past the white faces

of lost men, who stared, gaping.
One man, hit by a stove, grasping

for something, swung his legs around the belly
of another stove sinking beside him

and rode it to the bottom.
When it settled in silt,

he slipped off—an arm floating across his forehead—
and slumped, exhausted, near the hearth:

wreck of a boy in November
done with chores.

J. OSWALD BOYD, 1936
Lake Michigan

After the tanker ran aground on Simmons Reef,
small boats gathered for days,

crowding like piglets near a sow,
suckling fuel—900,000 gallons—

as the hull of the ship
rose and fell

with each swell of the lake,
as though almost breathing.

The men in the boats cut their engines
when they approached.

They stubbed out cigarettes
in the sludge of old coffee

and took what was not theirs to take.
Beneath the glare of the sun,

they rode their boats like hog lice,
mange mite, wood tick, stable fly,

every man a vector of disease, bloated
but still thirsty.

DECKHAND: SOUND THEORY

Dishes rattling in the galley,
slap of water on hull,

a high-pressure hose
scouring an empty cargo hold,

hiss of steam, wind
and steel, drone of engines,

vibrations of crankshafts,
hum of compressors,

turbines, motors, pumps,
boiler vents, fans.

At first he walked
through the bony labyrinth

of the ship
holding onto rails or walls,

tipping from one side to another
as the ship tilted left, right, up, down.

Now noise steadies him—
purr of what vibrates

through the hull and
into the pipes,

rhythmic and mechanical,
the orchestration

of a ship at work,
acoustics of equilibrium.

The fluid in his own ears
thrums with it.

MYRON, 1919
Lake Superior

Sometimes Anna made meals
for the men who repaired things
around the lighthouse.
She let them eat in her dining room,

which was not hers,
and let them stomp
through her hallway,
which was not hers.

Nothing was hers—not the tower
that rose from the sand
nor the house she kept
beside the tower.

This she felt most keenly
when she stood in the kitchen
and overheard the men swap stories—
tales of drowning and shipwrecks—

around the table where she normally ate.
After the men left, the house smelled
of tobacco and disorder.
If one thing felt like hers, it was

the phonograph in the parlor.
She loved how mechanics became
acoustics—how a needle absorbed signals
like a kind of wick, igniting the air with sound.

The night the *Myron* sank, she played
the phonograph continuously, afraid
to extinguish that music.
While her husband tended the lantern,

she pointed the horn of the gramophone
out the window, projecting ballads
in waves across Whitefish Point.
They touched places light could not reach.

CHARLES S. PRICE, 1913
Lake Huron

The oiler holds a white towel, wonders where
to press it. For one year, before his father got sick,
he studied medicine. He learned the names of bones:

malleus, incus, stapes, femur, tibia. He learned the names
of diseases: *diphtheria, tuberculosis, typhoid fever.*
He learned poverty and disappointment.

Nothing saved his father. Later, he had a new
vocabulary: *beam, ballast, bilge, boiler, bow, bulkhead.*
He thought if he studied these names, he could hold

the ship together. Nights he'd lie awake with lists
of words—one on the right, one on the left, trying,
in his head, to draw lines between them, connect boat

to body. As the steamer began to sink, he did not know
what to treat first—where to stop the bleeding or how
to fit a tourniquet to a whole hull. Now he kneels

on the deck holding the wet towel—useless compress,
old rag soaked with the sweat of his father's fever,
flag of surrender. *Sternum, bunker, femur, bowsprit.*

SUPERIOR, 1856
Lake Superior

Nothing belonged in the water
except the water, and even that churned

like water that didn't belong,
like water filled with too much

water. The crew, oilskinned,
slipped to lifeboats—

to shore, to shelter,
warmth, wives—

but their captain tried
swimming in a buffalo coat

greased with the oily residue
of a wild and ungovernable life.

The wool stiffened and froze
until the pelt was a clattering

wind chime: feral coda
for what had already died.

DANIEL J. MORRELL, 1966
Lake Huron

As a boy, he used to plunge
the bow of his schooner
into three-inch troughs,
storms he stirred into creation
with hands pruned from bathwater.
Later, his mother always came in
and chided him for the soap ring
he failed to scour from the tub.
Now his men are bailing
a 580-foot steamer,
his hands are useless, and he thinks
of the Ivory bar on the ledge
above his wash bin, the froth
and agitation of the water,
scum the soap will leave when it dissolves,
a ring his mother might recognize,
her eyes trained for such things.

PHOENIX, 1847

Lake Michigan

Lifeboats drop from davits
with the sort of recklessness
only known during disaster.

Seven passengers climb in one boat,
banging shins, scraping knees.
Water breaks over the gunnels.

The oars are lost. Women are trying
to paddle with the palms of their hands.
The boat is bobbing. Men are shouting.

One man from Wisconsin
sculls with a broom,
sweeping the immensity of the lake

over and over again,
as though he might make it
to a beach, a dry expanse

where he will brush away the prints
of plovers and write his name in the sand,
prove he is alive.

PEWABIC, 1865
Lake Huron

Books, spectacles,
an unfinished game of cards
on a folding table,
canned sardines,
crates of beer,
watches, pickles,
salted fish,
a hoopskirt packed in a trunk,
sarsaparilla, slippers.
Things made for living.

Revolvers from the Civil War.
Remingtons with top straps,
a Smith & Wesson
with brass cartridges,
a LeMat revolver: two barrels.
Caps, powder flasks,
a nipple wrench,
lead balls, various bullets,
grease, oil, ramrods.
Things made for dying.

Hard to categorize the water
they slipped beneath.
Put it on one list and it seeped
into the other, darkening everything—
walnut grips of handguns,
cotton cuffs of buttoned shirts,
tintypes of children left behind.

BREWSTER, 1943
St. Clair River

Water leaks into the hold,
leaks and slowly soaks 90,000 bushels
of lend-lease wheat
until the hold is a swelling belly
that expands as the wheat expands,
until what has swelled buckles the plates.
Soon the ship will sink,
the wheat will sink, the charts
charting the way to England will sink,
and the manifest manifesting the wheat,
cargo that is itself a manifestation
of expansiveness, will sink.
The crew will escape, so close
are they to Walpole Island,
so close to people with wool blankets
and hot coffee and Cream of Wheat,
bowls of Cream of Wheat
men will spoon into their bellies—
warm holds that will expand with gratitude
and some kind of fortitude
that kept people, in 1943,
from buckling.

DECKHAND: GAME THEORY

Some nights he plays cribbage
            in the galley with a wheelsman
from Duluth. The Formica table
            is a lake, the cribbage board
a boat. Each peg
            is a man moving fore to aft,
each card another boat
            docked against the lip
of the table—
            rim that keeps boats
from sailing off the edge
            of the world.

He plays the queen of hearts,
            remembering a valentine
he sent to a girl a dozen years ago.
            He'd printed her name,
Mary,
            above the queen's head.
It meant *take this, keep this,*
            play it against me if you want,
which she did.
            Now he docks the queen
next to the king of hearts,
            each boat rising with each
swell of the lake, each swell
            rising like what still rises
in his throat when he thinks
            of the girl.

The wheelsman plays
            the ace of hearts.
Ace of hearts, king of hearts,
            the deckhand wasted cards
in the spokes of his bike
            before he ever met the girl.
He spent afternoons cruising
            down to the ore docks,

twisting his handlebar grips
        as he peddled faster,
racing the Oswald boys.
        They punctured his tires
when he won.

He plays a six.
        The wheelsman plays a nine.
Fifteen for two.
        Six, nine.
What is a deckhand?
        Two,
which makes a deckwatch
        three,
which makes a watchman
        four.
Bosun, wheelsman,
        third mate, second mate,
first mate, captain.
        Five, six,
seven, eight,
        nine, ten.
And that is only the Deck
        Department.
Face cards he does not count—
        men in suits in front offices
on shore.

Now he's holding a jack
        and a five.
He thinks he should play
        the jack
if he wants to win.
        But if he irritates
the wheelsman,
        he's a boy
back at the ore docks,
        he's a young man
whispering a woman's name.
        Winning is losing,
and he wants to keep
        his boats safe,

count his fleet,
            put his peg back
in the soft flannel
            pouch for the night.

TWO HUNDRED FORTY-SEVEN SHIPS, 1926

Lake Superior

It is early December,
thirty-five degrees below zero.
Two hundred forty-seven ships
are locked in ice near the Soo Canal.
Men on shore hitch their horses,
pile meat and liquor onto sleds,
and set off to sell provisions to sailors.
Sailors walk across the ice to shore,
looking for tobacco and girls.
Almost everyone crosses
back and forth, but others sleep,
or stare across blocks of ships,
expecting a neon theater marquee
or a streetcar. One deckhand wanders
alleys between hulls of boats,
longing for a post office or a library
or the schoolyard where he might find
his daughter playing Fox & Geese,
her red scarf flapping in the wind
like a small craft advisory.

LADY ELGIN, 1860
Lake Michigan

For an hour, he stuffed canvas
into a hole in the hull,
trying to seal the leak.
It was like packing a wound.

He knelt in water and probed the orifice
with cold fingers, feeling his way up
into the hollow
where water rushed.

Deckhands tossed cargo overboard
and tried to drive cattle off the side.
The cattle were terrified and suspicious.
They huddled together,

the ship listing dangerously with their weight.
He wanted to abandon the gaping hole,
the useless plugs,
and stand with the cattle,

solid creatures
who had no capacity to think
ahead, only the instinct to congeal
into a mass of quivering flesh.

HENRY CLAY, 1851
Lake Erie

Baled wool washed ashore for weeks.
At first, the appearance of each bundle
was sobering and macabre,
but after a few days, one woman
began to look forward to the surprise
and the wealth
of what drifted her way.
She ripped the jute bags
and pulled out the stuffing—wet, still
scented with grease and mystery.
She dried the wool, carded it, spun it,
wound it into skeins,
and made scarves and sweaters.
Sixteen men died when the ship sunk.
At least something would come
of the cargo they carried—
mittens for the children of friends,
caps for five nephews.
Sometimes, she wondered why
bales floated and men didn't,
and what buoyancy meant
for her own life,
dry as it was.

WILLIAM NOTTINGHAM, 1913
Lake Superior

When they ran out of coal in the hoppers,
he moved wheat from the cargo hold
to the bunkers, and shoveled it
into the firebox as though slopping pigs.
It burned—salvation and waste—
and he shoveled more, thinking
of his dad feeding horses
and his brother scattering seed for chickens.
He flung the last handful to the wind
and watched it fall, imagining
how it might bob on the surface of the lake
and drift to shore and blow over several counties
and land in Gladstone and sprout next spring:
thin green hair that would grow and thicken
and feed the cows grazing at home.

HATTIE TAYLOR, 1880
Lake Michigan

After the deck was loaded,
the crew listened to water
lapping against the hull:
gentle slap, whispered taunt.
The men made their silent requests,
amending old appeals for wages
or women, and asking, now,
only to make it across the lake.
The schooner was top heavy—
too much wood on the deck.
The men were uneasy, imagining
the load sliding, the force of waves,
pressure on the boat's ribs.
When the storm came,
they felt everything shift—
the lumber, the deck, the frame.
Wood, rigging, a barrel of flour—
all of it washed over.
The men took to a yawl.
Later, they watched a salvage
crew raise the schooner
by pulling on the mast—
oak that snapped like a wishbone,
conceding nothing
but its splintered remains.

FRANCISCO MORAZAN, 1960
Lake Michigan

Only last week it was still
October: high cumulus clouds
and something gentle in the air.

Now waves pummel the hull
and sleet lashes his face.
He thinks of the woman he met

that night the ship docked in Chicago—
the straps he slipped off her shoulders,
her dress, which slid to the floor.

Linoleum. Waxed, slippery.
He wants her, or he wants
what came after her: a coffee pot,

yellow curtains,
three oranges in a red bowl,
a ball game on the radio,

a dresser for his wallet,
a rug beside the bed, a geranium
on the kitchen windowsill.

Maybe, most of all, the geranium,
which was not too dry
and not too wet,

and smelled of the earth—
soil and chlorophyll
and roots.

J. BARBER, 1871
Lake Michigan

Peach crisp, peach pie, peach jam, peach compote, whole peaches, sliced peaches. In those hours before the peaches burned, the whole ship smelled like August in a farm kitchen. The hold was full of Michigan orchards, full of juice and sugar and the soft fuzz of peach skin. The fuzz burned first, singed like eyebrows too close to a candle, and soon the skin shriveled, but not before each peach was seared, the sweet juice of summer briefly concentrated and contained before everything cooked, oozed, dripped, and exploded. Peaches sizzled and spit as the ship burned, as fire consumed what was made of sugar and what was made of wood, as masts toppled like limbs pruned from fruit trees, as men rolled across the deck like windfalls, bruised and scraped, and everything was reduced to carbon and loss.

DECKHAND: DREAM THEORY

He falls into sleep
headlong, as though into water.
Every night a sudden descent,
his body spread, weightless,

striped pajamas
ballooning near ankles.
His feet: white,
pale as bone under moonlight.

Some nights he flips on his back,
flutter kicks the sheets,
drifts until his brain waves
slow, his heart settles.

Whatever comes to him
in that stretch of deep
sleep—a sturgeon bigger
than the ship, a storm—

whatever comes,
he keeps breathing,
the rise and fall of his chest
as rhythmic as the boat.

WALDO, 1913
Lake Superior

The passengers have made a fire
in the captain's bathtub
and are gathered around it,
eating tinned peaches with their fingers.

After they burn the legs of the washstand,
and after the tinned fruit is gone,
few things remain
to tether them to this world:

one door to the pilothouse,
ripped from its hinges
by three deckhands,
one life jacket,

which sits like the last peach
no one will eat,
one megaphone
a woman holds quietly in her lap

like a sleeping baby.
She strokes it gently,
as though silencing a wild holler
hiding inside.

SIDNEY E. SMITH, JR., 1972
St. Clair River

He was at the wheel of the *Smith*
that day in Port Huron
when the bow got caught in the current,
pushing it into the path

of a downbound steamer.
A few weeks later,
he heard a barber speak of guilt
as though it were an insect.

Endless stridulation, he thought,
as the barber tilted the razor
away from the lump near his throat.
That summer was full of unsteerable days

stitched together with the relentless rasp
of insects.
He saw in the bodies of brown field crickets
the hulls of tiny ships

and heard in their rubbing body parts
the ceaseless grind of metal on metal.
He spent nights on his porch drinking Stroh's,
trying to steer the sounds of insects

away from the home where his son slept
beneath deep blue blankets,
and where his wife drifted in cool sheets,
her hair fanned around her

as though underwater.
He thought everything was sinkable,
and never heard the music
of what was still afloat.

COLUMBIA, 1859
Lake Michigan

They dropped anchor at Plum Island,
but when the chain broke they lost
what held them—all that was taut and fixed.
Slammed into shore, even language splintered.
They climbed into the rigging
of the double-masted brig
like spiders, and moved from rigging
into tree branches like birds
and lived thereafter with a knowledge
of what was inside them: silk
and spinnerets, wing bars and tail feathers,
extra lives wrapped in sailcloth.

J. R. SENSIBAR, 1939

Lake Michigan

Wind ironed oilskins to the backs of men,
worked like women's hands,
churned the lake into a foaming washbasin,
spritzed the faces of men, slick with rain,
and blew spray into eyes
and drove water up noses,
blew the freighter onto the shoal
and left it stranded,
left the crew limp and soaked.

On the beach, the Coast Guard
prepared a Lyle gun
to send a rope from shore to ship.
Someone collected a bucket of water
from the lake
and doused the shot line
so it would not burn
when the black powder exploded,
firing the projectile and the line.

After the line was sent and secured,
the men on the freighter ran a whip line
through a pulley block,
and when all of the ropes were anchored
from ship to shore,
the crew took turns slipping into a buoy,
each man hanging,
legs flaccid, arms limp.
The wheelsman went first, followed by the helmsman,
followed by the oiler and three deckhands.
On shore, men reeled them in,
counting faces as white as sheets.

MATAAFA, 1905
Lake Superior

The captain waded through flooded passageways,
his shins pushing against water,
his feet slowed by a current that kept growing.
The last of the kerosene lamps burned out,
the matches wet, the rags wet,
and he waded as he waded rivers
on moonless nights, waiting for holes
to swallow him, wary of snags.
Still, water poured in, a fluent stream
bent on mutiny, and the captain waded
through it, against it, fleeing in clothes so wet
they clung to him like leeches.
In darkness, he groped for the simplest thing—
dry tinder, something to help him see
what was left of the governed world:
pilothouse and portholes and the pale flesh
of his men, still bailing the surging
insurgent waves. He questioned
if he ever commanded anything—
the wheel, the galley, the deck, the men,
the ever-rising uprising.

ST. LAWRENCE, 1878

Lake Michigan

A Four-Color Process

C.

In the galley, ▓▓▓▓

▓▓▓▓▓▓▓▓▓

▓▓▓▓▓ fire

▓▓▓ ignited

▓▓▓▓▓

▓▓▓▓▓

▓▓▓▓▓

▓▓▓▓ their clothes

▓▓▓▓

▓▓▓▓▓▓▓▓

in ▓▓▓ quick sizzles.

▓▓▓▓▓

39

M.

████████ a kettle

of ████████

████████

████████

████████

████████

People dove into

the water, ████

flaming

Candle stubs ████

████████

████████

Y.

pitch boiled

over and

A ship

dipped

in a trough:

K.

caught

from tar warmed

to seal it

before darkness.

The Proof

In the galley, a kettle

    of pitch boiled

        over and caught fire.

A ship ignited

    from tar warmed

        to seal it.

People dove into

    the water, their clothes

        flaming.

Candle stubs dipped

    in a trough: quick sizzles

        before darkness.

INDEPENDENCE, 1853
Lake Superior

The crew clung to bales of hay,
flotsam once meant to feed the horses
in mining camps on the Keweenaw.
One sailor laced his fingers around baling twine
and pressed his face into a bale,
smelling all of central Wisconsin after rain,
something sour and musty and born
of the earth. He dug his fingers
into the bale and swung his right leg
over it as though mounting a horse.
All night, he straddled the bundled mass,
remembering an afternoon in the barn
with a girl from school, his legs spread
on either side of hers, the way their sweat
coaxed a new scent from dust and dry hay.
He pressed his face into the bale
until what he inhaled became the mane
of his father's best mare, the hair
of the girl in the barn, the barn
in late June. Scent kept him alive,
gave him a reason to breathe.

DECKHAND: COLOR THEORY

He was green, just out of school,
and still had a boy's expectations
of color. Days on a ship, he assumed,
would be cyan and yellow—

blue water, a gold circle
fixed in a clear sky. A few afternoons
came close. More often,
the lake was the color of slate,

the sun, pale and weak.
Piss, they called it. No women
to scold the deckhands.
Mornings when the water was gray,

it looked hard, something
that could split your head open.
Real color was elsewhere:
red of rusting steel,

red of his own blood
rising in thin beads
when he sliced his finger
on a hatch cover.

Orange ring buoys. White lifeboats,
a kind of hope. Not enough.
Deep black of starless nights
and unventilated cargo holds

packed with coal and methane
and the threat of combustion.
Combustion: more red,
more orange, and something

close to yellow, but not the yellow
he imagined. All of it flashing
in sparks that sank in water
too deep for language.

CARL D. BRADLEY, 1958
Lake Michigan

The 623-foot limestone carrier is sinking.
He heard the deck buckle—
heard it groan and snap—
and heard the signal to abandon ship:
seven short blasts, one long.
There are men hacking at a steel cable,
trying to free a lifeboat,
men still waiting for orders,
men trapped below deck,
and men fumbling with life jackets.
He has only minutes to do anything—
pray, panic.
A button pulled loose, a coin tossed:
if he can discard as much of himself
as possible, there might be a trail,
a way back or a way out,
proof of his life.
He pulls shirt buttons,
which pop like rivets

sheered from the ship's hull,
pulls lint from his pocket,
and a jackknife he's carried for 14 years.
The crack in the ship is widening
when he pulls the ring his wife slipped
on his finger three years ago.
He flings it into the lake
and is sure he can see it spin as it sinks,
twisting into a double helix—
golden spiral staircase he will tumble down,
drowning all over again.

MESQUITE, 1989

Lake Superior

Freezer doors swung, unbolted. Ring bologna slid off the deck. Peas poured into the lake, plump and bloated as the eyes of drowned mice. Sliced white bread floated like lost manifests, pages torn from a logbook. Spinach leaves bobbed like water lilies. Orange juice blended with water until color disappeared. A two-gallon tub of egg salad plummeted: anchor without a chain. Potatoes sank like rocks. Steaks marbled with fat tumbled to the bottom and settled on ledges of red sandstone streaked with white veins.

OMAR D. CONGER, 1922
Black River

The Omar D. Conger *was docked in Port Huron, Michigan, when a boiler explod-ed. The ship was blown to pieces. A 200-pound radiator plummeted into the Falk Undertaking Parlors during a funeral service.*

Some said the radiator was a message from God,
which caused more than a few arguments.
Even among those who believed
in a radiant God capable of flinging
a heater through a funeral parlor,
there were some who said the coming
of the radiator was an expression
of God's solidarity with those who grieved,
and some who said the coming
was the beginning
of an eleventh plague.
Whether it was wrath or sympathy—
darkness or radiance—hardly made sense
to others, who claimed it was only
coincidence. But even some
who favored *coincidence* came to feel
differently about the word. They heard,
only, *coincide,* which they mouthed silently
to themselves, slipping in occasional
variations: *homicide, suicide, genocide,*
so many *cides.* For them, the lexicon
had changed. A word was redefined
by tragedy, and in certain families
in Port Huron, some smoldering remnant
of that day lives in the language
of those who survived the survivors.
For them, every coincidence
is a kind of death.

WISCONSIN, 1929
Lake Michigan

What he knew of death
was a brood mare in a barn stall
heaving quietly in the dark—
contraction and silence.

When the canvas on the lifeboats
hummed in the wind
and lanterns slammed against bulkheads
and fire-grate doors swung

on their hinges,
he heard music
and felt, only,
the excitement he remembered

when neighbors came
for threshing:
thrilling commotion,
cessation of monotony.

NAMELESS
Vessel Unknown, Date Unknown
Location Unknown

Stranded, he clings to a clump
of rock cress, stroking the basal rosette
as though fingering the hair of a woman.
The leaf is shaped like a lyre
and when he touches it, he listens
for music, something to sing him to sleep
now that the waves no longer rock him.

He's walked the beach, has seen dune thistle,
tickseed, ninebark, cinquefoil,
bulrush, harebells, things
that might keep him alive.
He's recited the shapes of stems and leaves,
and what he remembers of blossoms.
He thinks if he burns bearberry leaves,
evil spirits will stay away.
Later he is uncertain,
thinking only of what the wrong smoke
might do to his lungs.

One day he collects woolly sedge
to make baskets and twine
and wad into wicks for lights,
but he does not make anything.
He thinks he could brew coffee
from the seeds of beach pea, and boil
cattails to eat like corn on the cob.
He stands on the beach saying,
beach pea, beach pea, beach pea,
forgetting coffee,
forgetting corn on the cob.

When it begins to rain,
he collects tall stems from shallow water

and weaves a little house of bulrush,
saying all of the names
of all of the beach plants
over and over, waiting for one
of them to say his name, *Henry,*
in some delicate, lacustrine voice
as soft as fringed gentian,
as sweet as meadow fern.

ALPENA, 1880
Lake Michigan

When apples bobbed in the surf
after the wreck of the *Alpena*,
she waded out in darkness
as though entering a play
in which gauzy clouds became a Greek chorus
singing a story of a ship and a storm
and a promised future. She listened
and thought of all the boys
who left her, and of the rot in her core
some had palpated and tried to name.
When the clouds parted,
she lifted her skirt, bent down,
and dipped her face into the lake,
trying to sink her teeth into the white flesh
of a Pippin or a McIntosh
and, in the sinking, claim her berth
as the next to marry.
She knew of this custom,
borrowed from Romans and Celts,
and when fruit floated to shore in October
and clouds sang to her,
it seemed a sort of destiny.
Out of disaster would come matrimony, she thought,
as she scooped the reflections of old stars
into the hem of her skirt—
white veil she would raise
again and again
for a man who was floating to her
on the lid of a lost piano.

DECKHAND: WORD THEORY

All of those vocabulary tests in school
meant nothing. Everything
was indeterminate. Take *collide*,
those two *ll*'s parallel, but no,
not parallel, that is the problem,
parallel only in word, not world,
not fog, not gale. In the lake,
direct impact, violent crash.
Hard *c*, moment of contact,
ide, a chemical made up of two
or more elements, evidence
of a binary world, floating
versus not floating. *Ide*, end
of pride, end of *aide*.

Take *sink*, no, not the water basin
attached to a wall, porcelain noun.
Not even the infinite infinitives,
to descend, to weaken, to disappoint,
to drill, to dig, to defeat.
Those constructions can't get this right.
Listen to the *s*, air going out
of an inflatable raft, think about
in, *in* water, *in* ice, reconnect
the *s*, *sink* comes after *sin*,
hear the *k*, hard sound,
caw of gulls circling a wreck.

NOTES

Alpena, 1880

The *Alpena* left Grand Haven, Michigan, with a load of passengers and several railroad cars full of apples. After the ship disappeared, those apples kept washing up on shore, mostly near Holland and Saugatuck. Other things washed ashore too, including part of a stairway, part of a piano, lumber, and a water-soaked note signed by a man named George.

Brewster, 1943

Thirty-five men were aboard the *Brewster* when it collided with a 380-foot freighter. All of them were saved. The ship, a British freighter captained by a man from Scotland, sank six minutes after the collision, but in that six minutes the captain maneuvered the ship to shore. This probably made the rescue easier and also meant the *Brewster* did not block the shipping channel, a significant passage for war traffic.

Carl D. Bradley, 1958

Of the thirty-five men aboard the *Bradley* when she sank, twenty-six were from Rogers City. The 623-foot self-unloader was on its last scheduled run of the season. Even before that last run, the captain shared concerns about the boat's safety. It was full of rust, the ballast tanks leaked, steel plates were riveted (not welded), and rivets popped under stress. In the wind of that November storm, hull stress caused more rivets to pop. The ship kept sailing through the gale, but it twisted and sagged and eventually broke in half. Only two men survived.

Charles S. Price, 1913

The *Price* was one of twelve boats that sank in the great storm of 1913. Thirty-one more grounded on rocks or beaches. More than 250 men died. Lake Huron saw the worst of the storm. Eight boats were lost in one day on that lake. Bodies from the *Price* washed ashore in Ontario. They were laid out in the back of a furniture store so relatives or friends could come and identify them.

Chicora, 1895

When the *Chicora* made a January run between St. Joseph, Michigan and Milwaukee, Wisconsin, Lake Michigan was partially frozen. The shipping season was over, or supposed to be over. The boat made it to Milwaukee and was unloaded, stocked with coal, and reloaded with new freight. It left *Milwau-kee* about fifteen minutes before a telegraph message was sent to the docks, warning the captain not to sail because the barometer was falling. The ship disappeared. No bodies were recovered, but after the storm, searchers found a line of wreckage frozen in ice along the shore near Saugatuck, Michigan.

Columbia, 1859

When this double-masted brig got caught in a storm, the captain found refuge near Plum Island, but the boat lost two anchors and was pushed ashore. The crew climbed from the rigging into tree branches. A tug came to salvage the boat several days later, but a second storm had destroyed the brig.
The *Columbia* was the first boat that carried a load of copper from the Keweenaw Peninsula.

Daniel J. Morrell, 1966

This 600-foot steel freighter was upbound on Lake Huron in a November storm when it broke in half off the tip of Michigan's thumb. One man, Dennis Hale, survived thirty-six hours in a raft before he was rescued by a Coast Guard helicopter. Investigators determined the steel used in the ship's hull was too brittle. In fact, steel used in all ships built before 1948 was inferior. Above a certain temperature, the steel had some flexibility. In cold weather, it was likely to crack.

Erie, 1841

The *Erie* left Buffalo with a few hundred passengers (many of them Swiss and German immigrants) and a load of freight. An explosion caused by paint and turpentine started a fire, and the ship (wood, full of fresh paint) burned quickly, fanned by the lake breeze. Three boats arrived to help—the *DeWitt Clinton*, which saved about twenty-five people, and the *Lady* and the *Chautauqua*, which towed the burning ship to shore. The remains of the *Erie* sank while the two steamers towed her.

Francisco Morazan, 1960

The *Morazan* was a Liberian steamer carrying 900 tons of chicken, lard, and machinery when it got stranded off South Manitou Island in a late November gale. It's still there—a massive steel-hulled freighter coated with cormorants.

Hattie Taylor, 1880

This schooner got caught in a September storm near Sheboygan, Wisconsin. She was top-heavy with a deck load of wood, and she rolled on her side. The load fell into the lake, and the ship filled with water. The crew escaped in a lifeboat.

Henry Clay, 1851

The *Henry Clay* was headed from Detroit to Buffalo with a load of flour and wool when it got caught in a gale. The load shifted and broke the engine, and waves tore the deck from the hull. One deckhand was saved, picked up by a passing schooner. Twenty years before this wreck, the ship left Buffalo with 370 soldiers headed for the Black Hawk War. That trip ended with a cholera outbreak.

Henry Steinbrenner, 1909

The *Steinbrenner* was downbound in a snowstorm in the lower St. Marys River when it collided with an upbound freighter. It was carrying 7,000 tons of iron ore. The ship was raised and returned to service. It sank again in 1953 in Lake Superior during a gale.

Independence, 1853

The *Independence* was the first steamship to run north of the Soo. In 1845, the 118-foot boat was portaged around the rapids at Sault Ste. Marie with the help of wooden rollers and a horse. It took seven weeks to move the boat one mile. (Hard not to think of Werner Herzog's *Fitzcarraldo*.) In November of 1853, on her last scheduled trip of the season, the boiler exploded when the ship was a mile out of the Soo. The *Independence* sank almost immediately. Four people died. About thirty people survived.

J. Barber, 1871

The propeller *J. Barber* was on its way to Chicago with a load of fruit when the steamer caught fire. It's believed the fire started from rags hanging near a hot pipe. Two people died. The ship sank about ten miles off Michigan City, Indiana.

J. Oswald Boyd, 1936

This tanker was hauling gasoline when it ran aground a few miles northwest of Beaver Island in November. For two months, people took their small boats out and helped themselves to free gas. This went on until the salvage rights were purchased by the Beaver Island Transit Company. The company sent a boat, the *Marold*, which pumped out 20,000 gallons on her first trip. On its second trip, the *J. Oswald Boyd* exploded while the *Marold* was pumping gasoline. Nobody survived.

J. R. Sensibar, 1939

The 600-foot freighter was being towed into Grand Haven, Michigan, when gale-force wind broke an eight-inch hawser and set her adrift. The U.S. Coast Guard was able to rescue the men on the *Sensibar* without putting a rescue craft in the water. This incident marked the last time the Breeches Buoy was used in the Great Lakes. Several years after this event, the *Sensibar* was captained, for a few years, by Ernest M. McSorley, the man in command of the *Edmund Fitzgerald* when it sank in 1975.

L. C. Waldo, 1913

This ore carrier was near the tip of the Keweenaw Peninsula when it got caught in the great storm of 1913. The storm pushed the boat against the rocks of Manitou Island, broke the windows in the wheelhouse, ripped off the roof, destroyed the ship's compass and her electrical system, and snapped the rudder from the ship. The captain and crew made their way from the stern to the bow, holding the wire cable railing along the deck. They walked 300 feet in gale winds with thirty-foot waves crashing over the deck. Later, they huddled in the windlass room and hoisted a signal flag up the foremast. The chief engineer dragged a bathtub into the room and directed the crew to build a chimney out of fire buckets. Eventually, a rescue party found them.

Lady Elgin, 1860

This 250-foot passenger steamer was headed from Milwaukee to Chicago with a party on board. Leaders from one of Wisconsin's militias, the Union Guard of Milwaukee, had organized an excursion on the *Elgin* as a fundraiser to buy new weapons. The ship left Milwaukee in bad weather, but despite wind and danger, a band played and passengers danced. The schooner *Augusta* was also out on the lake that night, headed toward Chicago. The second mate on board the *Augusta* saw the mast of the *Lady Elgin,* and the second mate on the *Elgin* saw the mast light of the *Augusta*. Neither man was particularly concerned. By the time the *Augusta's* captain issued orders to turn the ship hard to starboard, it was too late. The *Augusta's* jib boom tore into the port side of the *Lady Elgin*. Water poured in, the *Elgin's* engines dropped through the bottom, and the boat broke into three sections. Passengers clung to wreckage. Some drifted to shore. Students from Northwestern University waded into Lake Michigan to rescue people.

Mataafa, 1905

The wreck of the *Mataafa* was so famous that a storm and a cigar were named after it. The storm of November 1905 is known as the "*Mataafa* Blow." Many ships were wrecked in the storm, but the *Mataafa* is famous, in part, because crowds witnessed the disaster. Shipwrecks don't always have an audience. This one did because the *Mataafa* turned back for Duluth during the storm and tried to "shoot the chutes" of the Duluth piers. People lined Canal Park and watched a wave slam the *Mataafa* into the north pier. The boat lost power and steering, and it tossed in the waves until it was beached about 600 feet from shore. Twelve men were in the stern, and twelve in the bow. Three men made it out of the stern and into the (safer) bow before the *Mataafa* split in the middle. The nine men left in the stern died. The fifteen men in the bow lit lamps and fires to stay warm. The crowd in Canal Park built bonfires on the rocks to watch the disaster. The men in the bow were rescued the next day. Bodies in the stern had to be cut from ice.

Mesquite, 1989

In December of 1989, the 180-foot *Mesquite* was pulling out buoys on Lake Superior when she ran aground off Keweenaw Point in shallow water that had, earlier, been marked by one of those seasonal buoys. The boat pounded against the rocky shoal and was wrecked. Later, the Coast Guard sank what was left to create a dive site.

Myron, 1919

The *Myron* left Munising, Michigan, in November with a crew of eighteen and 700,000 feet of lumber. She sank in a gale off Whitefish Point. The captain ordered his crew into lifeboats, but he stayed with the *Myron*. The pilothouse separated from the boat when the *Myron* sank, and the captain drifted on that wreckage until he was saved. The crewmembers died. Local residents chopped eight bodies from the ice and buried them in a cemetery in Bay Mills Township.

Omar D. Conger, 1922

The *Omar D. Conger*, a ferry that ran between Port Huron, Michigan and Sarnia, Ontario, was docked in the Black River at Port Huron when a boiler exploded. The boat was blown to pieces. Several pedestrians were knocked to the ground, thrown some distance from the docks. A 125-pound valve from the engine room crashed through the roof of a store, and a nearby house was destroyed.

Pewabic, 1865

Four months after the Civil War ended, the *Pewabic* collided with her sister ship, the *Meteor*, and sank near Thunder Bay. More than 150 passengers were on board, including many Union soldiers. The ship also carried a heavy cargo of freight, including copper ingots and ore.

Philadelphia, 1893

The 236-foot steamer *Philadelphia* sank after a collision with the steamer *Albany*. The wreck is mostly intact, as is the cargo, which rests on the deck and is scattered on the bottom of the lake next to the hull. The wreck is part of the Thumb Area Bottomland Preserve in lower Lake Huron.

Phoenix, 1847

The steamer left Buffalo with about 300 passengers—most of them immigrants headed for Milwaukee. Somewhere offshore Sheboygan, Wisconsin, crewmen noticed smoke and traced the problem to the boilers, which were so hot they set fire to the woodwork. Fire spread quickly, as did panic. Bucket brigades didn't work, and there were not enough lifeboats. Only about twenty-five people survived.

Rouse Simmons, 1912

Many captains extended the sailing season to earn more money, and many captains hauled Christmas trees during this extended season. When Herman Schuenemann bought the *Rouse Simmons*, he hired lumberjacks to sail with him to cut his trees. His brother, August, once had his own boat—and his own lumberjacks and Christmas trees—until both August and his schooner went down in a storm in 1898. Herman bought the *Simmons* after his brother's death and died the same way.

St. Lawrence, 1878

The schooner *St. Lawrence* caught on fire when a kettle of pitch boiled over. The captain and a passenger tried to launch a lifeboat, but both men fell overboard and drowned. The schooner *Granada* was nearby, and her crew saved four members of the *St. Lawrence* crew.

Sidney E. Smith, Jr., 1972

The *Smith* was upbound on the St. Clair River near the Blue Water Bridge when a call came in on the radio from a downbound freighter. The wheelsman made some adjustments to prepare for their passing, but the bow of the *Smith* was caught in the current, and the current pushed the bow downstream. The second mate blew a string of short blasts to signal danger, but the other wheelsman couldn't stop his ship. The downbound freighter struck the *Smith* so hard it rebounded, then hit the *Smith* again. Both hits punctured the *Smith's* hull. The crew made it off the boat, and about twenty minutes after the collision, the *Smith* sank, blocking the shipping channel. Since that wreck, the Coast Guard has not allowed simultaneous downbound and upbound traffic in that section of the river.

Superior, 1856

The *Superior* was a wooden passenger and freight steamer that was caught in an October gale in Lake Superior. The captain made a run for shelter off Grand Island, but the ship lost her rudder, the cargo shifted, and the boat was driven ashore near Pictured Rocks and destroyed in about fifteen minutes. Sixteen passengers and crewmembers made it ashore. Some found shelter in a cabin near Munising. Eight crewmen climbed onto the boat's paddle wheels, but they slipped off and died.

Two Hundred Forty-Seven Ships, 1927

Five thousand sailors were stuck with their boats in an early December freeze near the Soo. It took ten days of icebreaking to free most of the ships. Some weren't freed until the following April.

W. W. Arnold, 1869

This schooner left Marquette bound for Cleveland in early November with 550 tons of iron ore, two passengers, eight crewmen, and a captain. Several hours after her departure, the *Arnold* met gale winds, plummeting temperatures, and snow. She never made it to the Soo (a necessary destination to access the lower lakes). A month later, a mail carrier whose route followed the shore reported that he'd seen a boat beached near the mouth of the Two-Hearted River, about twenty-five miles west of Whitefish Point. Several members of the Masonic Order in Munising set out to search for the captain's body. What they found is detailed in the poem.

William Nottingham, 1913

The *Nottingham* had 300,000 bushels of grain in her hold when she was caught in a gale. The captain pointed the bow into the storm, which required the ship's engine to run at full throttle. He understood the storm would outlast the fuel and tried to make a run for shore. When he knew they wouldn't make it, he ordered the crew to pull off the hatch covers and scoop buckets of wheat to burn. The ship made it to Whitefish Bay but got stranded on a sandbar. Waves pounded her, and when some crewmen tried to launch a lifeboat, they were killed. Those who stayed on the *Nottingham* were saved days later.

Wisconsin, 1929

The *Wisconsin* was a freight and passenger ship that ran between Chicago and Milwaukee. She was built in 1881 and served as a convalescent hospital during World War I. The ship sank in heavy waves in an October storm with a load of iron castings, automobiles, and boxed freight. Some reports say nine people died, some say sixteen people died. Close to sixty passengers were saved. The wreck is about six miles southeast of Kenosha, Wisconsin. Machinery and cargo are still on the bottom of the lake, as well as three automobiles—a Hudson, an Essex, and a Chevrolet.

A Note on Sources: This information was culled from a variety of books and sources, including, most particularly, Dana Thomas Bowen's *Shipwrecks of the Lakes* (Freshwater Press, 1977), Dwight Boyer's *Ships and Men of the Great Lakes* (Freshwater Press, 1977), Robert J. Hemming's *Ships Gone Missing* (Contemporary Books, 1992), Cris Kohl's *The Great Lakes Diving Guide* (Seawolf Communications, 2001), William Radigan's *Great Lakes Shipwrecks and Survivals* (William B. Eerdmans Publishing, 1977), Benjamin J. Shelak's *Shipwrecks of Lake Michigan* (Trails Books, 2003), Kimm A. Stabelfeldt's *Explore Great Lakes Shipwrecks* (Stabelfeldt Publications, 1992), and Mark L. Thompson's *Graveyard of the Lakes* (Wayne State University Press, 2004) and *Steamboats and Sailors of the Great Lakes* (Wayne State University Press, 1991).

ABOUT THE AUTHOR

Cindy Hunter Morgan teaches creative writing and book arts at Michigan State University. She is also the author of two chapbooks: *The Sultan, The Skater, The Bicycle Maker*, which won The Ledge Press 2011 Poetry Chapbook Competition, and Apple Season, which won the Midwest Writing Center's 2012 Chapbook Contest, judged by Shane McCrae.